UNSTOPPABLE STEPS

UNSTOPPABLE STEPS

WHOSE SHOES
ARE YOU WEARING?

Angel Ker-Jefferson

TP TYROPUBLISHING Inc.

DEDICATION

I dedicate this book to my "lifetime boy-friend", my husband Jamar. I love you boo, beyond words, with my whole heart. You have loved me unconditionally in spite of my past. You are my best friend, my ride or die, my confidant, my minister and an awesome provider and amazing father. You wear your many hats extremely well.

Thank you for believing in me, encouraging me and supporting me babe! You are the best husband a girl could ever have!

Love you to Life!

ACKNOWLEDGEMENTS

Thank you Lord for your unfailing love towards me, you have been so good to me, even when I wasn't good to myself. I am forever grateful, so I choose to spend the rest of my life serving you with a grateful heart.

To my children...Justin, Jamar Jr. and Jajuan. You guys are the best, y'all are my sunshine on a cloudy day. I thank God for the opportunity to be your mother.

To my Spiritual parents...Bishop LA & Elder Lisa Wilkerson of Agape Christian Ministries. Thank you for your words of encouragement, pouring your wisdom into me and teaching me the Word of God in a way that I can easily apply it to my life and the lives of others... You are TRULY the greatest of all times!

There are many people that without their love, prayers & encouragement this book would not have seen the light of day. Thank you so much, I pray God blesses you abundantly!

PREFACE

This book is intended to propel young women to discover their ordained identities. We were all created for a specific purpose and oftentimes we jump off track, especially if there is no one there to teach us the right way. I believe God allowed me to endure yet survive all the experiences and obstacles that I faced so that at this moment in my life "For such a time as this"... I can be a blessing by pulling someone out of the pit they are headed into. I am telling my story through a character because often in my life, I felt like I was someone else.

Parental advisory is suggested, the content moving forward may be a little graphic. It is heated truth, but if we don't expose what's REALLY in the fire and make the decision to pull our girls out of hell's destruction..... WHO WILL?

Make no mistake; my book is not a platform to support teen sex, drugs, mischief and deceit. However, it is a window view into my life and is centered on restoration, healing and total transformation.

FOREWORD

This book is not a typical story about a woman's life. It is a testimony of triumph, resilience and resurrection. It can be used as a map to help women navigate through some of the toughest storms that life can bring their way. The brave transparency of Angel in this book demonstrates her desire to see others become overcomers.

As a Pastor, I have seen countless numbers of individuals suffer some of the most horrendous situations but not many like the one Angel made it out of. To me, she transformed the title of being a " Katrina victim" into being a "Katrina Victor!" Somehow, she was able to beat death and one of this nation's most horribly catastrophic storms to still emerge with the purest-kindest heart I have ever seen. Her storms of life did not make her bitter, they made her better.

This book has inspired to me to help others look at life's most ugly "set backs" and allow God to use them for "set-ups".

Bishop L A Wilkerson

Author of The Making Of A Leader

Unstoppable Steps: Who's Shoes Are You Wearing?

Author
Angel Ker-Jefferson

TYRO Publishing & Media Services
http://www.tyropublshing.com

Cover Design by
Darrel Francis,
Brand One Logo & Designs

INTRODUCTION

Macy Toussaint was a charismatic and fun loving child. She had brothers who looked after her, a father who loved her and a best friend whom you couldn't tell her wasn't her sister. But, there was something dark inside of Macy that was yearning for something; during her childhood years of ages eight to eleven, Macy had some things happen to her that she was not proud of; she was often fondled by someone in her family. Although there was never any sex involved, there was inappropriate touching, that often left her confused about what was going on. Macy knew that what he was doing had to be wrong because he told her not to say anything...but she did! Macy tried to tell her parents but that didn't go over well. They sat her down and said "Now don't go around saying stuff like that, you can start a lot of unnecessary problems in the family." In other words, they didn't believe her, so from that moment on; she felt like she could never go to them again. In fact, she told no one else…but because of that shameful encounter something had awaken in her that was irresistible. She became curious. The lifestyle of the girls in her neighborhood was intriguing.

Macy lived in a 2 parent home and went to a nice Catholic school with real morals and values but still something was always missing. She searched and searched, she couldn't find it in her parents, her mom was always away doing her thing, her step-dad was an older gentleman, and although he loved her and the ground she walked on…she couldn't talk to him. He only saw her as "baby girl". Her biological dad was not involved because of a step-mom who hated her.

She couldn't find it in her family because they were so judgmental, so she began looking for it in her friends. As time progressed, she saw something that was intriguing to her about the girls who hung out by the local store. They seemed to be happy all the time, the boys always followed them wherever they went, wore the hottest fashions, always had money...they APPEARED to have it all! Macy decided that she wanted THAT lifestyle! Macy was so eager to learn what to do to achieve THAT "lifestyle". She was naive, and had no street knowledge at all; but little did she know, she was about to get a crash course and grow up real fast! Things are NEVER on the inside as they appear on the outside. There is always a story, so "when you decide to wear someone's shoes; make sure they are the right fit! You may have to walk awhile!"

It will look as though Macy's life was headed for self-destruction, but there was a point in Macy's life when God stepped in and slowed her down! All was not lost and her story is surely a "...But God story!"

I pray this book will minister to you, your daughter, your nieces, your sisters and your friends. Ladies, nothing is too hard for God and IT IS NEVER TOO LATE FOR A TURN-AROUND! Our steps are UNSTOPPABLE because they were ALREADY ORDERED, we just have to surrender!

Don't worry about your past mistakes or time wasted, it was never wasted, remember...there are lessons in everything!

Besides, Joel 2:25 says that "God will restore the years...!"

Blessings to you!

CONTENTS

Chapter One

STILETTOS
{TOO HIGH, TOO YOUNG}

Summer of 1989 in New Orleans, Louisiana...When the term "daddy's little girl" was devalued for 13 year old Macy Toussaint.

In most homes the term Daddy's little girl refers to the doting father who covers and protects his daughter at all cost. The image of a huge, handsome and loving father sitting in his recliner with a shotgun in his lap, ready to pursue and pounce on any perpetrator who even thinks about or considers getting close to the little girl that he loves and keeps close to his side day and night. A daddy who kneels quietly by his baby girl as she quietly recites The Lord's Prayer and looks down at her lovingly, gently stroking her hair as she continues to drift off to sleep while all tucked into her decorative Strawberry Shortcake comforter. Finally walking away leaving his pumpkin alone sleeping peacefully as he closes the door behind, shutting off the light finally glancing backwards to assure his sweet daughter, the apple of his eye has drifted off sound asleep.

Forward winding to puberty when her little breast began to form and she notices her expanding hips as she gazes into the mirror. She did not feel like that beautiful, growing young lady standing in front of her, but this is the first time she noticed the need to finally let her mom know it's time to go bra shopping. **It's about time**! Macy had been waiting for this day her entire life, or so it seemed. There was just a tiny unsettling her belly as she looked longingly at that little girl inside of her that really desired to scream. She was not in a hurry to purchase a new bra, nor was she ready for any of the milestones that came with becoming a teenager.

Who's influencing the young girl in the mirror?

Shhh! Be quiet, my daddy will hear you! It's the night Macy made a bad choice to let Ronnie in her room at midnight; it was the night that fast tracked her life into a roller coaster ride. That night, she cried herself to sleep with blood in her sheets. There were so many emotions happening; she was in pain and she felt horrible about what she did, but she at the same time enjoyed it! The rush and the feeling she felt that next morning aroused an appetite for more. She believed this guy was paying attention to her, he told her that she was the prettiest girl in the neighborhood.

The evidence was staring back at her in the mirror.

Mirror, Mirror on the wall, who is the fairest of them all?

There was this place deep inside of Macy that never believed the answer the face inside that mirror beheld. It was much too simple to believe the truth, instead Macy desired a truth that did not exist, she accepted the cravings that deep pit in her stomach where her natural father was missing. This emptiness was her truth and there was nothing that could fill the desire of emptiness down deep where all secrets seem to be hidden.

Secrets are never free, there is always a price to pay!

When truth is desired but the thought of truth is never quenched. When young girls recognize this emptiness and there isn't anyone around to help guide them to the fulfillment they are longing for. Ultimately these young ones will begin to seek the closeness they are longing for with the attention and affection from anyone and everyone that will provide the few minutes of love, pleasure or desire, because after all a temporary fix is better than loneliness.

Once left alone, unprotected and ultimately violated Macy could not possibly attempt to understand all of these strange feelings on her own. Navigating through the variations of disgust and ecstasy all in one sweep is simply to much for a young girl to deal with. The warmth and comfort felt by being held and ultimately touched can become a sensory overload of such. The need for attention and the thought of a man's love replacing that longing for someone who was definitely not around can invite unwelcome towards an impressionable young woman just entering puberty.

Unfortunately there seemed to be no one else around that she could open her broken heart to; or she simply did not feel comfortable confiding in even those who were the closest to her. All of her material needs were met, but deep inside of Macy's soul she was wearing a pair of heels that were pretty but much too tall for her small stature to handle.

Stilettos can look amazing on, but girls like Macy who are not mature enough to wear them, instead of making a statement, serious self-injury can be lurking just around the corner.

I remember playing in my mother's high heels when I was a little girl, tap tap was the sound made on the floor. I was a cutie and had loads of fun playing in my mom's shoes in spite of their ill-fitting and my extreme clumsiness wearing them out of the house would have been impossible.

My mother knew to protect me; remaining close by she would have never put my life at risk while letting me wear those big girl shoes out of our home. Yes they were much too big for my little fee and as I tipped toed prancing around our house looking down with big smile taking pride in knowing someday I would be able to fill those shoes...but not yet.

On another occasion as I grew much older, I began to sneak out of the house wearing my sister's wedge heels. Being only 12 years old at the time in the 5th grade, my mother said absolutely not. I was not allowed to wear those outside of the house for the same reason she would not allow me to wear them outside years earlier.

As our daughter's grow and develop, they may also take dangerous risk making choices that are possibly life altering. Macy's choice earlier was surely life changing but it would not be the end of the world for her. If only she had made a better to choice by informing her mother, she could have possibly intervened resulting in turning the situation completely around.

Perpetrators begin to prepare their victims long before they actually commit the assault. Gaining trust and organizing a plan inside of their mind first, because the act of violence towards a child usually begins in the mind of the sick individual and by the time he or she makes one move to perform the act, they have executed their plan down to perfect hardly ever getting caught in the act.

For this reason alone it is important to openly discuss these types of situations with your children early on so that in the event they become a victim, they will have already understood this type of assault on their tender lives could ruin them long term. Macy's decision and failure to share her secret with her parents is the same reason many victimizers are hardly ever exposed for who they really are, while continuing to blend in society and perpetuating the same crime year after year going virtually unnoticed.

Many times we find ourselves making unfortunate choices that ultimately result in poor habits until we feel there is no turning back. As Macy begins to grow in God she finds her satiable appetite beginning expand to deeper depths desiring more of God and less of her former selfish behaviors.

As her unrelieved wounds begin the healing process, the pain ultimately goes away but the scar that is left behind is a constant reminder of never going back to that place of hurt again.

Scripture Meditation:

When I was a child, I used to speak like a child, think like a child, reason like a child; when I became a man, I did away with childish things. For now we see in a mirror dimly, but then face to face; now I know in part, but then I will know fully just as I also have been fully known. 1 Corinthians Chapter 13:11-12

Prayer Confession:

Heavenly Father, in the name of Jesus. I pray that my eyes are opened so that I am able to see myself the way you see me. I am the daughter of a KING! Amen.

Chapter Two

LEATHER VS. PLEATHER
{A SYNTHETIC LIFESTYLE}

That night, she began to see herself as pretty because he told her so... and she couldn't wait to tell the "girls" because she wanted so bad to be accepted in that circle. Little did she know, Ronnie was also one of the girls' boyfriends so her desire to be accepted was instantly met with opposition.

She was sold a dream!

What she thought was going to be fun was immediately starting to unravel, she began to isolate herself. (Trick of the enemy).

When you are left alone, *in your own head*! Your mind begin to play tricks on you...and that is what happened to Macy! She [enemy] began to tell herself that she was better than them, who did they think they were? So, now Macy battled daily, watching her back constantly, just to live this lifestyle that wasn't designed for her. She was not brought up this way, she insisted. But there was a stronghold she didn't know how to break loose of.

There was one girl in the group, Keeta; who believed that Macy didn't know Ronnie was Alicia's boyfriend. So, she began to hang out with Keeta a lot that summer. They became quite close, she even got her parents to start letting her spend nights at Keeta's house. Ms. Tina, Keeta's mom was super cool and was always dressed so nice, and always in a good mood. She would let Keeta catch the bus to Skate

Country, which was the popular hangout attend all the parties and dances at school, she got to hang out later than Macy could ever dream about. So one night during summer after coming in from a party, Ms. Tina was sitting in the living room with the music playing and singing loud; really enjoying herself. Macy asked Keeta if there was something special her mom did to always appear so happy. She said, *my mom enjoys life when she gets her fix, which is probably everyday*! So, Macy as inquisitive as she was, said "what do you mean, get her fix?" Keeta said, let me show you...*my mom is really cool. She lets me do it too.* So, she asked Ms. Tina if she could give me a taste, and she said "yes, but don't tell your mom and dad you got this from me". *That was Macy's introduction to marijuana.*

Always people pleasing and not knowing your value, will ultimately cost you more than you are ready or willing to pay!

What is your worth and how much would you pay to remain in a place called euphoria? Girls like Macy who are hurting always are seeking ways to numb the pain. Pain caused by the trauma in their lives, as a matter of fact, all pain can be traced back to some old trauma that was never reported or never revealed. Marijuana could not fix the pain, as Keeta's mom attempted to cover hers up with a phony experience but more sooner than later when she came down from that happy high, her numbing pain would be right there to remind her all over again of the traumatic experience of her past.

Trauma leaves clues if we look hard enough and long enough in the faces of those we love. Sometimes love can cause us to become blinded from the obvious truth that is many times the big elephant in the living room that everyone sees but pretends is not really there. The elephant grows more obtrusive causing a big stink and taking up space and indispensable unnecessary baggage.

Have you ever taken a trip and had more baggage than you needed and had to pay more for the space it would take up. There is a cost in our natural lives as well when we carry along more baggage than necessary, always seeming to drag that elephant around with us, pretending it is not there, and proudly whipping out the credit card to swipe our indecision away while we make every attempt to ignore the truth directly up front and center.

Leather shoes have a way of forming a snug fit around our feet and allowing us to maintain a level of comfort as our feet fit snugly inside the custom made shoe. But on the contrary a pleather shoe never it's very well. We go all day long enduring the pain of poor broken feet we have been dealing with over the last 20 years because we refuse to purchase a decent pair of leather shoes.

A nice pair of leather shoes will cost more to purchase and maintain over time. The longing to be a good fit, however never fitting in leaves a person always attempting to make relationships work, even the bad ones. The lesson in good material and bad material is quality and workmanship. It takes better material, and good craftsmanship in order to create a good pair of pumps that will not-only last for years, but will fit comfortably.

On the contrary, pleather shoes are usually quickly put together and are never a good fit. You are always looking for a reason to kick them off in order to give your foot some air. Leather shoes breathe. Relationships will fail to deliver as well in some cases, causing those that are the closest to us to begin to feel as if we are suffocating. When we hold in secrets and fail to even schedule the big reveal there are sometimes we may find ourselves holding our breath around those who are the closest to us. Signs began to come to the surface and we use excuses, arguments and indifferences to prevent us from having genuine conversations that would lead to the truth.

Revealing the truth must happen eventually, but at this time in Macy's life she was too fragile like that broken heel example earlier and instead of being real like the leather pair of shoes, she chose the synthetic lifestyle of making appearances and pretension.

Scripture Meditation:

The righteous cry, and the LORD hears And delivers them out of all their troubles. The LORD is near to the brokenhearted And saves those who are crushed in spirit. Many are the afflictions of the righteous, But the LORD delivers him out of them all.... He keeps all his bones, not one of them is broken. Psalm Chapter 34:17-20

Prayer Confession:

Heavenly Father, in the name of Jesus. I bind up the need to live a synthetic lifestyle, "for whom the son has set free is free indeed." Amen.

Chapter Three

COLORED BOTTOMS
{CAN YOU REALLY AFFORD THEM?}

Macy started sleeping over at Destiny's house quite often. Then, one night they were getting high and when they got in the bed to go to sleep, Destiny asked Macy if she ever wondered what it felt like to have her vagina tickled? Macy said, yea, she was hoping Ronnie would do that since she had been doing him. So, Destiny said let's put on some music so no one can hear us and see for ourselves. That night, opened a whole new area of sex for Macy. It was the start of something she had become addicted to, having to have this experience over and over again.

If you don't count the cost of the lifestyle you are coveting, you will soon find out that you cannot afford it.

Summer has come to an end, and Macy is now an 8th grader in a Catholic School with a huge appetite for sex and material things. The boys at her school could not provide the exploits she had become accustomed to over the past couple of months, nor could they fulfill what had become her desires.

Yep! Macy was now this new [synthetic] person who had the summer of her life, but little did she know it would be an expensive price to pay for a pair of the latest *colored bottoms.* Her sexual cravings could not be quenched and it did not matter to her at this point who or where they would be quenched by. Ultimately her past was holding on to her like a leach refusing to let go and sucking the life out of her.

Although she kept holding her breath, holding onto the secret pain and holding on to her past longing for love wherever she could get it, this craving would not leave her. Gluttony is a spirit that never gets enough and can never be satisfied. This satiety area inside only knows it wants to be fulfilled and by any means necessary.

Greed is temptation on steroids and together they cause the monster to get bigger, bolder and badder without any thought about how their disgusting behavior is causing others to feel around them. Hurt causes so much pain, but the agony of the pain is only left alone to desire the fulfillment of more and never enough. This pair of colored bottoms is expensive but it does matter to those who are hurting. If they have to spend their mortgage, car note or child's lunch money nothing satisfies until the desire is tamed, but only for a moment.

This unquenchable thirst for fullness in an area that can never be full has to be like living inside of a prison of some sort where it is impossible for the sun to shine. Screaming to get out, but comfortable with being fed and clothed, yet being told what to do and when to do it. You see sin is likened to a bully who is always waiting at the same corner so he can take your lunch money on the way to school, until one day you grow up big and stronger than the bully to ultimately experience the thrill of victory.

Those colored soles may be pretty on the outside and knowing the cost attached sometimes give the aura of importance and satisfaction; but eventually that bill will show up in the mail due upon receipt and if not paid in full the penalty will be insurmountable. Nothing can replace a need that only God can fill. Money nor expensive things can replace the time lost of losing the love of a father.

Wet kisses across the face setting off the senses of untapped desire ultimately climaxing yet leaving behind a feeling of guilt and regrets.

The stain of shame can hardly be removed unlike a bad tattoo that finally fades to green and the remembrance of it is forgotten caused by the color bleeding into the skin leaving behind what once was called body art is now only a blur.

Ultimately, Macy's poor choices and bad decisions put her on a roller coaster of regret bitterness and resentment, but at this point what did she have to lose. A temporary fix was better than no fix at all. The seducing monster kept calling her and it felt good. At this point nobody else was trying to ease her chronic pain, so she continued to answer until enough was REALLY enough.

Those shoes began to be too expensive, although they looked good while on, the price was entirely too much to bear alone. She needed a get out of debt plan that would eventually tame that monster of gluttony. After all enough was enough of covering these expenses alone. Macy needed to tell someone the truth, but who would listen anyway.

The bill was finally due and her bank account was in the negative. She had made far too many transactions for a young woman of her age. Her taste was too expensive, but fortunately for her God was always there waiting for her to take hold of his stretched out hand. His hand was always there, but she could not see it because of all of the sparkly expensive toys she desired. But still and quiet He stood there with loving eyes gazed upon her just waiting for her to look up.

Scripture Meditation:

When I passed by you and saw you squirming in your blood, I said to you while you were in your blood, 'Live!' Yes, I said to you while you were in your blood, 'Live!' "I made you numerous like plants of the Field. Then you grew up, became tall and reached the age for Fine ornaments; your breasts were formed and your hair had grown. Yet you were naked and bare. Then I passed by you and saw you, and behold, you were at the time for love; so I spread My skirt over you and covered your nakedness. I also swore to you and entered into a covenant with you so that you became Mine," declares the Lord GOD.

Ezekiel Chapter 16:6-8

Prayer Confession:

Heavenly Father, in the name of Jesus. I pray for that you help me make wise decisions, and to

stay in my lane going forward.
I choose to follow your lead.
Amen.

Chapter Four

WORN OUT SOLES
{INNER HEALING}

Macy was beginning to get bored, she began fantasizing and daydreaming in class so much that she began fantasizing about one of the counselors who was easily aroused by her gestures. He was, as the girls would say "weak for young meat".

By now, she was experienced at making things work to her advantage. She knew that in order for her to skip school so she could go be with her friends, she would have to give up something. She had the perfect plan, Macy not only developed an appetite for material things, she had an even bigger appetite for sex. It had become rhetoric for her, it meant nothing to her so she made a few passes at him to see if he would bite…and He did!

Breaking free from the bondage of promiscuity and low self -esteem into total freedom and confidence in God.

This once innocent little girl was now a vixen at 13 years old doing things grown women didn't do. My, My, My, how quickly time flies, so much has happened in a year she thought, as she sat on the steps of her house she thought, "it seemed like yesterday I was sitting here combing the hair of my doll!" She often wished she never went down that path but it was too late now because she couldn't turn it off [or so she thought]. She was not taught by example of how to be a young lady. Her mom spent a lot of time "doing her thing", so all she had was her friend's mom who was always there!

Someone told me that they don't EVER let their kids sleep out... I initially thought, wow, how much fun it could be for their kids. Then I was quickly brought back to my past. You know, I understand that as parents, we NEED a break; but at what cost are YOU willing to pay for that break? Is it at the expense of not knowing what can happen at another person's home? It is really important for us as Moms, Aunties, Sisters, Cousins, Teachers and Ministers to be that visible influence. That means getting our own act together. Yes, you may say, its survival, it happened to me and I turned out just fine, but I ask, *did you*? Or, you may say, that is not my child and if her parents are ok then it is not my business. I tell you, that [little] girl is longing for her rescue... her parents may not know, or they may not know how to help her because they were never helped. In some cases, it could be that [young] girl who is now 16, 18, 21 and even married, but was never rescued. *We are responsible spiritually to God for other people.*

There is a passage in the bible that talks about two brothers Cain & Abel. When Cain killed Abel and God asked, "Where is your brother? Where is Abel? Cain answered, "I don't know, Am I my brother's keeper?" Well, let's ponder that, shall we? God goes on to say, "What have you done? Listen! Your brother's blood cries out to me…"

When we let our girls die to this world, because we selfishly said "*it is not our business*" then their blood is on our hands.

Macy had become someone else. It wasn't long before she realized that the shoes she wanted to wear had become very uncomfortable. So now, just like a drug, when you can't climax on one, you move to another. Macy had become indulgent in skipping school and often felt like an outcast because she no longer felt like a normal teen, no one else in her entire class of 8th graders were skipping school. She often thought to herself how twisted it was to attend a catholic school that went to church every Friday, preparing for 8th grade Confirmation yet having sex in the lounge every Wednesday with a school counselor. In the ideal world, someone should have found them, then maybe she would have gotten help, Macy thought to herself. Maybe then, her parents would've listened to her or took her seriously.

HELP!! Is what Macy screamed silently...

> *"For none of us lives for ourselves alone, and none of us dies for ourselves alone" Romans 14:7*

Teen promiscuity is a serious matter today among many, because this matter should be of high importance on the radar of individuals or close to the victim but out of ignorance remain blinded by the very thing that is right in front of their faces.

Macy's impressions of her on value of lack thereof was an indication of her heart. You see God knows us and he sees our heart. We dress ourselves in the finest of clothes, expensive makeup and perfume, but when it comes to our feet many times we allow our shoes to wear out.

The failure to recognize what is right in front of our faces is the saddest position we often find ourselves in. Looking down at our feet to discover our shoes are worn out because of the miles of travel being victimized along the way. Many people who have been victimized by those they trust find it most difficult to discard old items. Because of this they will wear the same beat up pair of shoes that seem to be outdated. But if those who are closest would really pay attention to this one clue, they can eventually trace the date of the hurt.

Macy's shoes were worn out with a date that could be traced back to the night Ronnie crept into her bedroom. That particular night will always be engrafted on the flesh of her heart that is hidden from the very people who said they loved her.

Take some time out right now to discover an outdated pair of shoes inside of your personal closet. Check the date down to the very year. It doesn't matter if your offense happened in the late 70's, early 80's or even last year. You can trace the date because many who have been victimized remain right there at the place of their pain. Identifying the place and the date connected to trauma is strangely connected to those items that are found difficult to disassociate yourself with. You may find it quite hard and exhausting to discard those things; but if you seek the face of Jesus and leave those items on the altar along with the hurt and the pain. Eventually it will grow easier to separate from the experience and grow in maturity with a solid foundation in Jesus always.

There is nothing to difficult for God to handle. His specialty is healing and He came to heal the broken hearted. Simply ask Him to come into your heart and heal every area that hurts.

Scripture Meditation:

The word that came to Jeremiah from the Lord: "Arise and go down to the potter's house, and there I will let you hear my words." So I went down to the potters house, and there he was working at his wheel. And the vessel he was making of clay was spoiled in the potter's hand, and he reworked it into another vessel, as it seemed good to the potter to do. Jeremiah Chapter 18:1-4

Prayer Confession:

Heavenly Father, in the name of Jesus. I pray that you make me and mold me into a vessel to be used by you. Amen.

Chapter Five

BROKEN HEELS
{FINDING BALANCE ON
A ROCKY ROAD}

Finally, in her head, Macy figured that if she went into the confession booth every week she was good.

Her respective ritual with five Hail Mary's and one Our Father; very soon she would began skipping the booth and just saying the confessions. It never dawned on her that this adult was actually committing a crime and that there was so much more at stake, but she didn't care. Macy was so far gone into this character, she was lost. Now this appetite she had was turning into a unsatisfying hunger...a hunger that did not seem to be quenched.

Becoming mature and accepting responsibility of poor choices and seeking God for direction. Balancing a New Life, Motherhood and Marriage

The balancing act did not work very well with a broken heel. For some strange reason Macy attempted to visit the confession booth as a way to seek some sort of solace because this is how people in her circles cleansed themselves of secrets and innuendos. As a result they find themselves repeating the same discretion over and over again.

Sin has a way of calling us back to that same act that seem to always provide a temporary satisfaction that hardly ever goes away fully. This desire leads to a death, not just spiritual death as the bible mentions but a death to self and a death to having a meaningful relationship with God. God must turn his back on the act of sin, even when it means turning away from His own children. When Jesus was hanging on the cross and Holy Spirit departed from Him, God Himself also turned away from Him. Jesus must have felt alone, because He asked The Father, *why have you forsaken me? (Matthew 27:46)*

Similarly, Macy must have felt forsaken and all alone, because eventually her reckless behavior would catch up with her and she would eventually find herself in a confession booth that was one way in and no way out. All of us sin and fall short of the glory of God, because only God is good. Jesus even said, no one is good, not one but God.

Eventually Macy will come to grip with her present circumstances ultimately finding herself in a place where she has to face her fears. Stumbling through life with a broken heel will eventually grow tiresome. Hobbling up and down on one tiptoe and the other leg hitting the ground running and screaming for help from God. Eventually, growing tired of missing a heel on a pretty red pump that appears to be scuffed up and irreparable. The Shoe Doctor won't be able to help with this problem of self-infliction and self-mutilation. The only help in a situation like Macy's is finding the love of Jesus through a level of building a relationship that can never be separated by anything or anyone.

What is it that lingers inside of oneself that would cause a beautiful young girl such as Macy, with all innocence and purity intact one day allow a grown man into her bed the next? How does something like this happen right under the nose of adults sleeping in the adjacent room? Macy should have screamed, said no, but what really kept her from doing so? Instead she lay there accepting the closeness, the longing for love that apparently was not living at her address.

Macy is not alone, there are many more like her with similar experiences that are left confused and full of shame for many years. Some young women never get the

help they need and go on to live dysfunc-
tional lives. There seems to be a perpetual
curse that grows on all of the way through
family lines, penetrating one generation
after the next.

Soon Macy would have her own children
and will have to deal with her decision
someday. So many women carry this secret
to their graves, never forgiving the perpetrator but instead remaining the victim
avoiding telling anyone the secret they have
kept for decades. Many more of them carry
the pain like a fetus in vitro, the baby is still-
born and they cling to it even after infection
sets in causing them to be sick due to this
stinking tumor growing inside of them.

Broken heels can be repaired by profes-
sionals. Super glue and tape are quick
fixes, but brokenness requires a perma-
nent fix. The old Saints proclaim, Jesus can
fix it! Yes He is able to repair your heart,
soul and mind. Simply turn your problems
over to help and allow Him to carry you.

The calluses caused by the broken heel
causes a very hard layer of tough skin to

grow an overlay in order to protect your smooth healthy skin underneath. This extra layer of skin can be rough to the touch and sometimes painful as well as ugly in appearance. Once removed by a process of scrubbing and filing down the area, the end will result in beautiful smooth feet.

Take the time to study the word of God and allow the word to penetrate your heart, ultimately causing your heart that has been hardened by the pain to finally become softened and pliable for The Father's use. Only love from a Father can cause the calloused heart to become pliable, this love can be transferred down from generation to generation. Open your heart and allow Jesus to fix you, a process that takes time but is well worth the wait.

Macy's situation is far from isolated amid the questions and the whispers. She had her share of conversations ending once she walked in the classroom and laughter heard behind her back. But the opinions of her classmates was far from what Macy desired. All she really wanted was the love of a father and instead of getting the love she desired she often searched it out, but the outcome she would expect often left her lonely and hurting for the touch from anyone who was willing to spend time hold her close in their arms.

Searching for love is a normal human experience, but when that love is hardly found it becomes a trail of misunderstandings and innuendos that never cease. This painful trail goes on and on, and instead of walking away, like many other victims, Macy continued her search. Jesus says emphatically, *I love those who love me, and those who seek me find me. Proverbs Chapter 8:17*

Scripture Reference:

Nevertheless, the firm foundation of God stands, having this seal, "The Lord knows those who are His," and, "Everyone who names the name of the Lord is to abstain from wickedness." Now in a large house there are not only gold and silver vessels, but also vessels of wood and of earthenware, and some to honor and some to dishonor. Therefore, if anyone cleanses himself from these things, he will be a vessel for honor, sanctified, useful to the Master, prepared for every good work. 2 Timothy Chapter 2:19-21

Prayer Confession:

Heavenly Father, in the name of Jesus. I pray that my feet are planted on a firm foundation, Lord, clean me, create in me a right spirit and prepare me to do good works. Amen.

Chapter Six

GLADIATORS TO PUMPS
{TIME TO WALK THE RUNWAY}

Macy is now in high school, which was one of the worst high schools in New Orleans. She now faced competition, more temptations and ultimately a setup for disaster.

M acy was a wreck, she wanted to enjoy "high school" life but it was difficult because here she saw bigger things than just what her neighborhood had to offer. There were some real "Ballers" with real drugs and guns right in front of her on a daily basis. The temptations were extremely high.

You've always been dependent on someone else, and never really walked alone; well, now it's time to walk with purpose, become bold and confident and see yourself as God sees you.

Macy did her best to achieve success at masquerading her life; she often became exhausted by living this lifestyle. Macy was an all around socialite, on the dance team, in various groups, she was actually academically competent and knew she wanted something different for herself but she just could not turn this untamed craving off. She found herself in abusive relationships, trying different drugs, having sex with different guys that her body started wearing down on her by graduation.

By the time Macy graduated, she had tried every drug introduced to her. Because of her lifestyle, her reputation was horrible and she had lost many friends. She got hooked up with this guy that ran with a group who acted as a fraternity. Macy's entire freshman and sophomore years were spent smoking marijuana and having sex wherever and whenever available-from behind the school to abandoned houses. By her junior and senior years, she tried to turn some things around, but her preceding reputation made it hard for her. When she walked across the stage at graduation, she was actually booed by many of the female students.

In High School Macy was armed and dangerous as far as her classmates could see. They saw the tough armored exterior and the weapon was choice in her quick witted untamed tongue, but amid all of the noise, everyone around her missed the stream of tears falling down her cheeks and the bleeding heart inside of her that left small drips of blood behind as she would go from one bad relationship to another.

Another weapon Macy wore on her sleeve was her poor reputation among her high school classmates. They knew of her as the promiscuous girl going around sleeping with all of the boys and much worst, some of the teachers. Perhaps the rumors going around the school were in fact true, some false, but once a rumor fire begins to spread out of control, the possibilities of taming the whispers is close to impossible.

Soon Macy developed a touch outer shell and the rumors, whispers and stares did not seem to affect her anymore. She simply walked with her head high and pretended her haters were invisible, but it was her parents she was more concerned about, spending most of energy attempting to cover her trail so her parents would never know about her extracurricular activities. After all her mom and step-dad were the only stabilization she could count on in her world that seemed to be fraying at the scenes amidst her mountain of troubles she had begin to collect in such a short time.

Macy's behavior was not very accepted in the Catholic community, or at least it was not something done in the open. These types of secrets must be kept hidden and locked away. Open and intimate discussions about sexuality were not the norm, even if it affected an entire household, seeking council was not an option beyond the confessional booth. Solace was not a choice anywhere, so her only option at this point was to continue in the path she had chosen for herself.

God's path is sure, and although Macy seemed to be protected inside the confines of her home,, Catholic School and church family something had gone terribly wrong. Here she is now at a crossroad of her life, which path would she chose? The direction of her current location was a road to nowhere. But thank God for choices because many times we stray away from God's paths He has chosen for us and end up un an unfamiliar street and a dead end. Fortunately for us God will meet us right there at the dead end and throw us a rescue line so that we may eventually arrive at our ordained destination.

If you find yourself on the road to self-discovery and end up going in the wrong direction, remember to trust in God to shine the spot light on your situation. His light will even shine in a combat zone as you are on your way walking you life out wearing gladiator pumps. Prepare for your road ahead, which may be bumpy and your might just require assistance on your way. Remember weapons may be formed against you, but they will not prosper. (Isaiah 54:17)

Scripture Reference:

In righteousness you will be established: Tyranny will be far from you; you will have nothing to fear. Terror will be far removed; it will not come near you. If anyone does attach you, it will not be my doing; whoever attacks you will surrender to you. "See, it is I who created the blacksmith who fans the coals into flame and forges a weapon fit for it's work. And it is I who have created the destroyer to wreak havoc; no weapon formed against you will prevail, and you will refute every tongue that accuses you. This is the heritage of the servants of the Lord, and this is their vindication from me."

Declares the Lord

Isaiah Chapter 54:14-17

Prayer Confession:

Heavenly Father, in the name of Jesus. I bind up the spirit of fear, right now. I pray that I am able to walk as bold as a lion, no longer in competition by the world standards, but as one who has already won. Amen

Chapter Seven

COMBAT BOOTS
{A MISSION IMPOSSIBLE}

Macy's reputation followed her to college because so many people went to the same college. It had become very hard for her to make a fresh start, new friends, so she felt all alone.

Somewhere at the end of her 1st semester she met a guy, they became friends and then it turned into a relationship. This guy really liked her, he knew nothing of her past and she liked him too, but unfortunately he could not provide the things she was used to. Macy soon found a way to sabotage that relationship.

How often do we ruin relationships because of our own self destruction? We are so used to the "hard" and the "bad" that we can't handle the easy and good! What looks impossible to us IS ALWAYS POSSIBLE WITH GOD.

She knew she broke his heart and she felt bad but there was something in her that she could not control. Old habits started coming back and she found herself dropping out of school and living life the way she saw it being done..."The Hard Way!" She embarked on an emotional yet entertaining roller coaster. Macy worked 3 jobs to make ends meet; she had several "boyfriends" to get the things she wanted. There was a "boyfriend" for every need and/or desire. That ride came to a screeching halt...Macy found herself pregnant at 19! *Oh God*, is what she said! I am not ready for this...At the age of 20, she gave birth to her 1st son.

She wasn't ready to be a mom, so she leaned on her mom for support [her mom became the mom] and Macy was OK with that! Her mom's health began to decline soon after, and she thought, I gotta do something with my life...

Moving forward a few years, she made another poor decision in her early 20's...

Macy got married! A choice made for all the wrong reasons:

▶ Everyone else was getting married...

▶ Maybe this will fill that VOID...

▶ Maybe this will change me...

▶ My son will have a dad...

After being in an abusive marriage [verbally & mentally], she decided to GO BACK HOME and put an end to a bad decision.

Macy didn't know what she was in for...

Her husband could not handle the breakup, He told her "nobody could have her if he couldn't". She was threatened, stalked and then she became fearful. This went on for a couple of years, she was always looking over her shoulder. She couldn't afford to get a divorce [she felt like she was in a losing battle]. It got so frustrating, the turmoil seemed to be too much to bear. Macy found herself in a state of depression, life as she knew it wasn't fun anymore. The depression grew heavier and heavier, she cried countless tears, until she heard whispers of "leaving this world", "nobody will miss you", "you didn't do anything good anyhow" so she started drinking heavily...She needed a drink to wake up and function, a drink to "calm her nerves" in the evening and a drink to lay down at night. One night, Macy got so drunk at a club that she woke up the next day not knowing how she made it home, her car was half on the street and half on the sidewalk. It was then, she said "I can't do this anymore", it's time to end all this!

Does any of this sound familiar? We oftentimes make decisions out of desperation. What we don't know is that those decisions are EXPENSIVE!

Macy wanted so badly to end her life... At the age of 26, she tried to commit suicide, ingested some pills, she inhaled a bottle of alcohol...NOTHING! She thought, why is this not working? As she proceeded to look for a razor blade, her phone started ringing, not once, not twice...three times! High as a kite on pills and alcohol, she answered...

Hello!

Hey, what are you doing?

Why?

Just asking, something told me to call you. Hey, I want you to come with me somewhere tomorrow!

It was at that moment, there was a stillness. It was as if the call came through her cousin's number but it was God on the phone. She said, "I found this new church and I want you to come with me." Macy agreed, and her life was never the same!

After going through the journey, and you now see YOU! What is the next step? Seek-

ing God for direction on how He wants to
be glorified through your story...

The journey to self-discovery can be a long
and challenging road traveled. Many parents
have sent their rebellious sons and daugh-
ters off to boot camp because somewhere
down the road of adolescence they did not
grasp hold to discipline. Instead of waiting
out the bumpy ride, these parents decided
ot take massive action out of fear that their
children could end up going down a path
that could be a place of no return.

Unfortunately for Macy her parents did
not intervene soon enough because although the signs were there, they missed
it somehow. That huge neon sign on the
door of her heart kept flashing but no
one seemed to notice it. The calls from
teachers, the warning from noisy church
members, and even the neighbors who
they ran into at the grocery story tried
to scream out something is wrong in that
house but I just can't seem to put my
finger on it. So instead of saying exactly
what was on their minds they just zipped

their lips and made idle small talk while Macy was living in a combat zone on and her battle field was in her mind, while her personal life was on high alert.

What happens in combat when everyone around you seems to ignore the signs that are simply in place to warn us of the dangerous conditions? There are wire booby traps and grenades filled with poisonous gas being thrown from the enemy on every side. The weapons of mass destruction has still not been uncovered but though all of the signs noted present danger was close by, nothing was done to prevent the disaster that occurred right in the safe house of her own.

The military calls it friendly fire when a country's own troops cause injury or even death to its own. For some reading this passage, your personal family members that reside inside your own home have been attacked by a friendly fire of sorts. Could it be a cousin, uncle, father, or brother that caused Macy to endure friendly fire? Someday the truth may be uncovered but until then we must remember to tell the truth about our past because it's past time for a reveal.

A reveal occurs when the victim finally decides to share their personal secret information they have been coveting for years. This is a very difficult event for most because of fear their love ones will not believe their story especially if the perpetrator is close to the family. For every person who keeps a secret, ten more victims may be left suffering from abuse from the same person that caused harm to that individual. Unfortunately for some of you may not have the network of support as others, this is why joining a support groups such as a church or other organization can help. There is something about strength in numbers that help many people share their story with others over time.

The military protects its own and so does every enemy camp. The victim is often portrayed as if they are the responsible party in the first place. On the contrary, this is a problem area in some communities, especially some church communities. Failure to expose the truth, must come to an end once and for all. Make a decision to tell the truth once and for all. Once the truth comes out in the open, healing can take place for everyone involved.

As we travel during this journey to self-discovery, we may begin to see ourselves learning that we are much stronger as we begin to grow and prepare ourselves to share our story with others. Help is available; don't continue to ignore the hurt especially when so many have the same story to tell. There is a saying, "hurt people, hurt people", and there may be some ounce of truth to this statement because statics show victims usually grow up and become victimizers.

The time is now to stop the madness within your generation, stopping the assault on children and adults for that matter because the madness has to stop with everyone who reads this book. When children are victimized it damages them physically, mentally and spiritually in most cases.

Once the damage has been done, it may take decades to recover. Pay attention to your children verbal as well as nonverbal cues. If your child was once outgoing and is not reserved, this is the time to begin the dialogue with them and if they refuse to share, dig deeper. Sometimes the defensiveness or rejection can be a serious sign the child has something to hide. Most importantly follow your hunch or discernment; usually these feelings are a warning to us that there is a problem.

(Disclaimer: The information in this book is not meant to provide mental health or medical treatment. The information shared is based solely on my experiences and please take consideration to seek professional medical advice. The author is in no way presenting the information shared to readers as an all-inclusive method because every individual is different.)

Scripture Reference:

Finally, Be strong in the Lord and in His mighty power. Put on the FULL armor of God so that you can take your stand against the devils schemes.

Ephesians Chapter 6:10-11

Prayer Confession:

Heavenly Father, in the name of Jesus. I pray that you send your Angels that are assigned to me to war on my behalf. I trust you, Lord that this mission is not impossible and that the battle is already won. Amen.

Chapter Eight

FLIP FLOPS
{LIFE AFTER "THE JOURNEY"}

At this point, Macy is developing well and doing much better. She has grown up to become a wonderful wife and mother. She has begun to minister to others in the area of pain that she has suffered. Dealing with abuse and sexual addiction can both be very difficult experiences to share in public, but when multiplied with drug addiction as well; it can be a triple threat to remain healthy after keeping a secret so long and now finding the strength to let go.

Walking in Peace and Confidence by "just being you"

There is power in numbers and the more victims stand victorious the better it will be to make a commitment to remain a force to be reckoned with. Abuse must stop and the only way to do that is exposure.

Whenever God is ready to expose a situation, He simply speaks to it saying, Let there be light. Once light exposes the situation darkness must go. Darkness and light cannot remain in the same space. Therefore the actions of the enemy will remain exposed and abuse will decrease in our communities when more victims are speaking up and out.

Macy is now married with beautiful children and does not look like what she has been through. Whenever she shares her story with others, her listeners cannot believe these things could have ever happened to her in the first place. Through giving her life to God and placing her past in His hands Macy has found balance in her life.

Life will flip on you, but God is always consistent. Walking by faith can be difficult for someone who has always done thing their own way, but just as Adam and Eve was walking in the cool of the day and God begin to call Adams name, asking him the question...Adam where are you? Most of us know this scripture by heart but unfortunately even with this knowledge, Adam and most of us will only have excuses for God when he comes back again.

Flip flops are usually summer sandals worn by those who are trying to stay cool on a hot summers day. These are the best accessories and the greatest shoes next to wearing none and going barefoot on the cool grass or walking on the sand at the beach. Can't you just feel the stimulation under you feet and feel the coolness of the wet sand.

Flip flops also make lots of noise letting everyone know you are coming before your reach your destination. God knows what you have done, there are no secrets as far as He is concerned, because it's a matter of your heart. Once Macy dedicated her life to Jesus she gave Him her hardened heart and He gave her a brand new one.

Once Macy received her new heart, she begin to see life through a new set of lenses and new there was a better path to take then where she was going. Because of the love of God, she no longer had to go looking for love, love was always there. Jesus is love, and He was always with her the entire time.

One walk with God beats a million steps with anyone else. Walking with God makes your steps virtually unstoppable. You experience a freedom to go anywhere with the understanding there will be no barriers because God has already gone before you to make you way smooth and when God reveals your future there is absolutely no one who can stop your arrival date.

Without a doubt, there may be detours and roadblocks, but remember no one goes on a long journey wearing flip flops. This is your season to relax in God, because where you are going from this point on, only God can get you there. Never again will you need to wear shoes that don't quite fit, when you can simply enjoy the freedom and peace of being you. *You are Unstoppable.*

Scripture Reference:

Oh, what joy for those whose disobedience is forgiven, whose sins are put out of sight. What joy for those whose record the Lord has cleared of sin.

Romans Chapter 4: 7-8

Prayer Confession:

Heavenly Father, in the name of Jesus. I just want to say THANK YOU for loving me, for watching over me and protecting me; not only from others but from myself. When I didn't know you were there, you were ALWAYS there. I love you Lord, I love you Lord, I love you Lord! And I will bless your name at all times! Amen.

DECLARATIONS

I declare and decree that I am no longer bound to my past.

I declare and decree that I am FREE to BE ME!

I declare and decree that unforgiveness no longer reside in me.

I declare and decree that I am blessed and everything I touch is blessed.

I declare and decree that I was created to prosper.

I declare and decree that every unclean thought is no longer apart of me.

I declare and decree that the spirit of poverty, entitlement, and bitterness has been uprooted from my life.

I declare and decree that I am renewed.

I declare and decree that I am a child of the Most High God.

I declare and decree that I am BIGGER than my past.

I declare and decree that my Faith in God has been restored.

I declare and decree that my mind is on the things of God and no longer twisted.

I declare and decree that my health, mind and finances are restored.

I declare and decree that the peace of God shall reside and take precedence in my life.

I declare and decree that I am Fearfully and Wonderfully made, I am a Designer Original.

I declare and decree that the power and authority of the Lord is in me.

I declare and decree that I am no longer fearful.

I declare and decree that every good thing is from the Lord and it is flowing into my life.

I declare and decree that I am a distribution center for the things of God.

I declare and decree that the blessings and favor of God is stalking me.

I declare and decree that every void has been filled with the purpose of God.

I declare and decree that my life is new, nothing lacking, broken or missing.

ABOUT THE AUTHOR

A woman after God's own heart. Angel's passion is to propel women and teens to unlock their purpose in the Kingdom of God. Through God's grace, she has conquered a life that was setup to leave her stagnated or better yet, die. The calling on her life is to empower, edify and equip women of all ages to be effective in every area of their lives (Family, Ministry & Business). She is charged to Ignite & Inspire you to shake off a life of mediocrity and live as a designer original! It is her heart's desire to be a Woman of Integrity as she strives daily to become a Proverbs 31 woman and a servant God can trust!

Married to her Boaz for 9 years. They have 3 sons: Justin (17), Jamar Jr. (9), and Jajuan (5).

Angel is In pursuit of reaching all of her goals and dreams which includes her business, Kingdom Ladies Apparel and the highly anticipated publishing of her first book, Unstoppable Steps.

AUTHOR CONTACT INFORMATION

To request Angel Jefferson to be a part of your next conference or event, Or if you would like to order more copies of the book, please send your invitation and/or request to Living2InspireU@gmail.com.

www.ingramcontent.com/pod-product-compliance
Lightning Source LLC
Chambersburg PA
CBHW071159090426
42736CB00012B/2379